EDGE BOOKS™

THE KIDS' GUIDE TO

COLLECTING STUFF

BY CHRISTOPHER FOREST

Consultant:

David I. Schoeneman,
President of the
Illinois Pawnbrokers Association

CAPSTONE PRESS
a capstone imprint

Edge Books are published by Capstone Press,
151 Good Counsel Drive, P.O. Box 669, Mankato, Minnesota 56002.
www.capstonepub.com

Library of Congress Cataloging-in-Publication Data
Forest, Christopher.
  The kids' guide to collecting stuff / by Christopher Forest.
     p. cm.—(Edge Books. Kids' guides)
  Includes bibliographical references and index.
  Summary: "Describes different collectible items, including how to get started
collecting, where to find collectibles, and how to display collectibles"—Provided
by publisher.
  ISBN 978-1-4296-5442-5 (library binding)
  1. Collectors and collecting—Juvenile literature. 2. Hobbies—Juvenile literature.
I. Title. II. Title: Guide to collecting stuff. III. Series.
  AM231.F67 2011
  790.1'32—dc22   2010036883

Editorial Credits
Mandy Robbins, editor; Kyle Grenz, designer; Eric Gohl, media researcher;
    Eric Manske, production specialist; Karon Dubke, photographer

Photo Credits
All images from Capstone Studio, except:
Public Domain/United States coin image from the United States Mint,
    cover (coin), 9 (all)
Shutterstock/alexRem, 17 (bottom); ARENA Creative, 5 (top); Cameilia, 14 (left);
    Cappi Thompson, 8 (top); dedek, 16 (bottom); Dr. Margorius, 28 (bottom);
    Gemenacom, 26 (bottom); Jeff Banke, 12; Laenz, 27 (top); pashapixel, 27
    (bottom); Tyler Boyes, 17 (top & middle)

Printed in the United States of America in Stevens Point, Wisconsin.
092010   005934WZS11

Table of Contents

BECOME A COLLECTOR

Do you like looking at the designs on different stamps? Do you enjoy collecting trading cards and sharing them with friends? Do you spend time saving state quarters and storing them in coin albums? If so, you are already a collector.

Collecting is a fun hobby. It can help you organize your favorite objects and learn more about them. Many people also enjoy the challenge of adding new items to their collections.

There are so many items just waiting to be collected. Read on for fun tips that will help you build collections to last a lifetime.

Fun Fact:

A library is more than a room full of books. It's a type of collection. You can build your own personal library by starting a book collection.

Perhaps you have some lying on your dresser or jingling in your pants pocket. You know what it is—spare change. That change may be more valuable than just the number **engraved** on it.

Getting Started

Check your change regularly for old or unique coins. Old coins are often more valuable than newer ones. You can also look for **commemorative** coins like state quarters.

engraved—when a design is cut into metal, wood, or glass

commemorative—a type of coin that celebrates an event or person in history

What Makes a Coin Valuable?

Different factors determine the collectible value of a coin. Rare coins are worth more. Older coins are usually rarer. But some coins were created in small amounts. They are rarer than older, more common coins. Demand plays a role in a coin's value too. If a coin is in high demand, collectors will pay more for it. A coin's value is also affected by what it is made of. If the price of gold goes up, a gold coin becomes more valuable.

Finally, the condition of a coin affects its value. Coins are made, or minted, at a place called a mint. If a coin appears brand new, it is in mint condition. A coin in mint condition is worth more.

Fun Fact:

The first coins were made in the Middle East almost 3,000 years ago.

Organizing Your Collection

Some people sort coins by type. You might group all your pennies together, all your nickels together, and so on. Other people prefer to collect coins by years. They display a penny, nickel, dime, and quarter for each year.

Displaying Your Collection

Most coins can be stored in coin albums. These albums are three-sided folders. Collectors often protect very rare coins in glassine envelopes. These clear envelopes protect coins from water and air, which can make coins dirty and dull-looking.

MYSTERY OF THE DOUBLE EAGLE

The United States 1933 $20 Double Eagle coin is one of the most valuable coins in the world. These coins were the last Double Eagle gold coins ever made. All but two were supposed to have been melted down. But someone within the mint stole some. The Secret Service retrieved most of the stolen coins. The only Double Eagle coin made available to the public sold for $7.59 million in 2002. The buyer kept his identity secret. No one knows where this valuable coin is now.

Stamps aren't just for letters. Many people enjoy collecting stamps for their designs and the history behind them. There are stamps featuring movie stars, animals, presidents, and more. Governments from countries all over the world make many types of stamps. Some even come in different shapes, like triangles.

Fun Fact:

Musician John Lennon, of the famous rock band The Beatles, collected stamps as a child. Since his death in 1980, his face has appeared on many stamps.

Getting Started

Look for interesting stamps on your letters and postcards. Then trim the stamps carefully from the mail. You can also purchase new stamps from the post office.

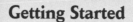

Organizing Your Collection

People often collect stamps that fit into a category. Some collectors look for stamps from all over the world. Others prefer to collect stamps based on a topic, like sports-themed stamps. A few collectors categorize their stamps by shape.

THE BIRTH OF
STAMP COLLECTING

England issued the first stamps ever made in May 1840. They quickly became a hit with collectors. According to the *London Times*, the first stamp collector was a British girl. In 1841 she placed an advertisement in the newspaper asking people to send her their stamps. The girl wanted to use them as wallpaper.

Fun Fact:

Stamps commemorating the 400th anniversary of Christopher Columbus' trip to America were printed in 1892. Some are worth more than $1,000 today.

Displaying Your Collection

You can purchase stamp albums from department stores, craft stores, and bookstores. You could also buy a stock book to hold even more stamps. These books have sheets of small stamp holders. Some stock books come with stamps already in them. For rare stamps, you might want to purchase clear glassine envelopes to protect your stamps. Some people collect and frame mint sheets of stamps. These are small sheets of printed stamps you can buy at the post office.

Some collections cost a lot of money. But a rock collection is free, and you can get started in your own neighborhood.

Getting Started

Once you've searched your neighborhood for interesting rocks, you can branch out. Any time you take a trip, bring back rocks. Beaches, forests, mountains, hills, and grasslands are good places to look. You can check out hobby stores or museum gift shops too. They may sell unique rocks.

Displaying your Collection

Some collectors shine up their rocks in a rock tumbler before displaying them. Others leave them in their original state.

Show off your collection in a shadow box from a hobby or craft store. These glass-topped boxes are ideal for storing rocks of all shapes and sizes.

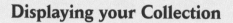

SHADOW BOX

GEMSTONE COLLECTION

Obsidian

Leopard Skin

Crystal Quartz

Tiger Eye

Zebra Marble

Malakite

Aventurine

Topaz

Chalcedony

Grey Agate

Jasper

Turritella

Diorite

Pyrite

Chrysocolla

Getting Organized

Some people prefer to organize rocks by size or color. Other collectors put rocks together according to the place the rocks were found.

Fun Fact:

Geodes are great additions to your rock collection. They are hollow sedimentary rocks with crystals inside.

Perhaps the most common way to organize rocks is by the three different types of rock. They are igneous, sedimentary, and metamorphic. Igneous rocks are formed when melted material from the Earth's interior cools. Examples are pumice and obsidian.

OBSIDIAN

Sedimentary rocks are formed by layers of sand, plants, or other materials being pressed together. These rocks include coal and sandstone. **Fossils** are usually found in sedimentary rock.

SANDSTONE

Metamorphic rocks are made when heat, pressure, or liquid reacts with sedimentary or igneous rock. The structure of the original rock changes, creating a new type of rock. Marble and diamonds are examples of metamorphic rock.

DIAMONDS

fossil—the remains or traces of an animal or plant from millions of years ago preserved as rock

Baseball cards have been a hit with collectors since the late 1880s. They started as a cardboard backing for cigarette packages. Baseball cards are no longer part of packaging. Now they are sold for their own value.

Getting Started

Department stores, sports stores, and some toy stores sell baseball cards. You can purchase small sets with a few cards or large sets with every player on a team.

Look for cards of players who broke important records, like Ted Williams, Hank Aaron, or Cal Ripken. The value of a baseball card is usually based on the player and the condition of the card.

THE MOST FAMOUS BASEBALL CARD

In 1909 the American Tobacco Company released what would become the most famous baseball card ever. It was the Honus Wagner T206. The story goes that Wagner, a Pittsburg ballplayer, disliked smoking. He asked the company to stop producing his card. The company agreed, but not before 50 to 75 cards were released. In 2007 a Wagner card sold for $2.8 million!

WAGNER, PITTSBURG

Organizing and Displaying Your Collection

Be sure to keep your cards safe from wear and tear. Some stores sell card albums that can hold plastic sheets. Several cards fit in these sheets. Other people purchase plastic cases to hold cards. Some collectors organize their cards by teams. Others group cards by year.

Comic books first appeared in the 1930s. Since that time, both children and adults have enjoyed reading and collecting them.

Getting Started

Most people start collecting comics because they enjoy reading them. Start your collection with a few of your favorite titles. Then try to find different **editions** of the comics. You can buy comics at comic book stores, pawnshops, or antique stores. You can search the Internet as well.

edition—a number of copies of a comic all published at one time

Organizing Your Collection

Most collectors group comics by title and keep different editions together. Some organize comics by themes, such as superhero comics or video game comics.

Displaying Your Collection

Comics are most valuable when they are clean and their colors haven't faded. Keep your comics in plastic sleeves. You can buy these sleeves at hobby stores. For extra protection, place cardboard behind each book.

Fun Fact:

When *Action Comics* was first published in 1938, it cost a dime. The first edition featured Superman for the first time. A first-edition copy sold for $1 million in 2010.

Spiderman, Batman, and Superman are not just comic book heroes. They are also action figures! And believe it or not, some of them are worth a lot of money. The value of a collectible action figure depends on its condition, rarity, and popularity.

BATMAN
THE BRAVE AND THE BOLD

BATTLE AXE
BATMAN
FIGURE

4+

AGES 4+

INCLUDES
3 FIERCEST
FOES
BATTLE CARDS!

SPIDER-CHARGED GLIDER
SPIDER-MAN

SPIDER-MAN

Getting Started

Many people start collecting action figures as children. Others start collecting as adults as a way to remember their childhood. Collecting action figures is definitely a fun way to stay young at heart. Department stores, toy stores, pawnshops, and even thrift stores are all great places to find action figures.

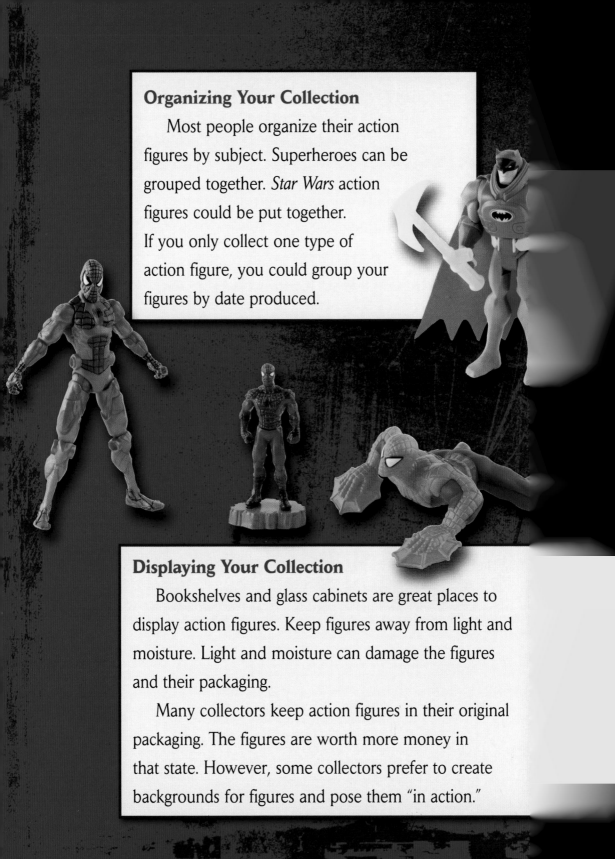

Organizing Your Collection

Most people organize their action figures by subject. Superheroes can be grouped together. *Star Wars* action figures could be put together. If you only collect one type of action figure, you could group your figures by date produced.

Displaying Your Collection

Bookshelves and glass cabinets are great places to display action figures. Keep figures away from light and moisture. Light and moisture can damage the figures and their packaging.

Many collectors keep action figures in their original packaging. The figures are worth more money in that state. However, some collectors prefer to create backgrounds for figures and pose them "in action."

AUTOGRAPH COLLECTING

What's in a name? To an autograph collector, a signature may be as valuable as gold. Whether you're interested in movies, sports, or music, autograph collecting is an exciting hobby. It can even bring you face-to-face with people you admire.

Getting Started

Collecting autographs requires persistence. You have to be in the right place at the right time. You may also have to wait in long lines. If you want an athlete's signature, head to a sporting event. If you want an author's signature, look for book signings at local bookstores. Many collectors even write to their favorite celebrities asking for autographs.

Organizing and Displaying Your Collection

Some people collect signatures in autograph books or notebooks. Autograph books make great coffee table decorations.

Other collectors have celebrities sign items such as tickets, books, or CD cases. Autographed items can be shown in a display case.

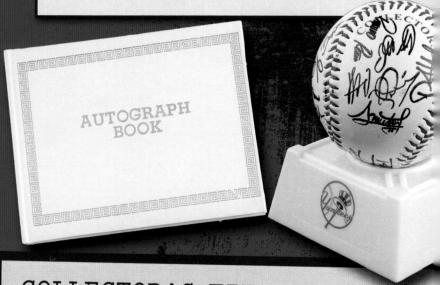

COLLECTOR'S TIP

Many autographs are purchased after the person who sign the item has died. In these situations, collectors have to worr about **forged** signatures. Some of these fakes are so good that they fool everyone but the experts. If you ever have a questio about a signature that is being sold, wait before you buy. Che with a signature expert before you make a purchase.

OCT 1 2 2011

forge—to make a fake signature

COLLECTING MUSIC

Do you scour the Internet to find the best new music? Do you load up your iPod or MP3 player with the hottest new tunes? Then you are a music collector.

Getting Started

Music collecting is easy, but it can get expensive. Music can be purchased through online downloads from legal sources. Some collectors also go to hobby shops, yard sales, or music stores. There they find old records or CDs for their collections.

Storing Your Collection

Most people store their music
collections in electronic players.
People who collect old LP records
store them in their original sleeve
containers. These records should
always be put in their paper wrappers
and stored on shelves.

Organizing Your Collection

Some people organize music alphabetically
by artists. Others store music by category. These
categories might include big band, rock music, pop,
and classical.

SOUVENIR COLLECTING

Do you enjoy traveling to different places? Bringing home souvenirs is a great way to remember your adventures. It's also a fun way to start a collection.

Getting Started

Any time you visit a place, bring something back to remember it by. Most vacation spots have souvenir shops. Popular items include magnets, spoons, and postcards. There are also plenty of free items you can find, such as napkins, matchbooks, or travel brochures.

Colorful Florida

Florida Alligator

Fun Fact:

Souvenir collecting became popular in the late 1800s. Around this time, Europeans began traveling for fun.

Displaying Your Collection

Keeping souvenirs in a shadow box is an easy way to show off your collection. Larger items can be put on a shelf for display. Some people keep a scrapbook to display flat items.

Organizing Your Collection

Organize your collection by trips. Dedicate parts of a shelf or notebook for each trip. You can organize your trips **chronologically**, alphabetically, or by location. One of the joys of collecting is that you can do whatever you want with your collection!

chronological–arranged in the order in which events happened

Glossary

chronological (kron-uh-LOJ-uh-kuhl)—arranged in the order in which events happened

commemorative (kuh-MEM-uh-ruh-tiv)—something made to honor and remember an event or an important person

edition (i-DISH-uhn)—a number of copies of a comic all published at one time

engraved (in-GRAYVD)—a design or letters that are cut into a metal, wood, or glass surface

forge (FORJ)—to make a fake signature

fossil (FAH-suhl)—the remains or traces of an animal or plant from millions of years ago preserved as rock

igneous rock (IG-nee-uhss ROK)—rock that forms when magma cools

metamorphic rock (met-uh-MOR-fik ROK)—rock that is changed by heat and pressure

sedimentary rock (sed-uh-MEN-tuh-ree ROK)—rock formed by layers of rocks, sand, or clay that have been pressed together

READ MORE

Orr, Tamra. *Coins and Other Currency: A Kid's Guide to Coin Collecting.* A Robbie Reader. Hockessin, Del.: Mitchell Lane Publishers, 2009.

Price, Pamela. *Cool Comics: Creating Fun and Fascinating Collections.* Cool Collections. Edina, Minn.: ABDO Publishing Company, 2007.

INTERNET SITES

FactHound offers a safe, fun way to find Internet sites related to this book. All of the sites on FactHound have been researched by our staff.

Here's all you do:

Visit *www.facthound.com*

Type in this code: 9781429654425

 Super-cool stuff! Check out projects, games and lots more at **www.capstonekids.com**

INDEX